First published in Great Britain 2023 by Farshore
An imprint of HarperCollins*Publishers*
1 London Bridge Street, London SE1 9GF
www.farshore.co.uk

HarperCollins*Publishers*
Macken House, 39/40 Mayor Street Upper,
Dublin 1, Ireland D01 C9W8

Match Attax is a registered trademark of Topps Europe Ltd.
TM & © Topps Europe Limited 2007

Images used under license from Shutterstock.com

ISBN 978 0 00 860357 1
Printed in the United Kingdom
2

Written by Kevin Pettman

A CIP catalogue record for this book is available from the British Library.

WELCOME TO
MATCH ATTAX ULTIMATE TRIVIA!

This **EPIC** book is bursting with **FOOTY FACTS** and **SUPER STATS** that will help you master the exciting world of **FOOTBALL**!

Discover the secrets behind every position on the pitch and what gives the game's superstars the edge over their opponents – then take on our **TOP TRIVIA QUIZZES** and **PRO PUZZLES** to see if you've got what it takes to lift the trophy!

Get ready ...
It's time for kick off!

GOAL MACHINES

DIFFICULTY: ⚽ ⚽ ⚽

Everyone loves goalscorers! They finish off fluid team attacks and some can launch long-range rockets. How well do you know the world's greatest forwards?

1 Who is the all-time top scorer in UEFA Champions League history?

- [ ] Paul Pogba
- [ ] Cristiano Ronaldo
- [ ] Lionel Messi
- [ ] Robin van Persie

2 What is the real name of Liverpool's legendary forward?

- [ ] Mohamed Halas
- [ ] Mohamed Salah
- [ ] Michael Salah
- [ ] Steve Salah

3 Who is the English top-flight league's all-time top scorer?

- [ ] Sergio Agüero
- [ ] Gabriel Jesus
- [ ] Alan Shearer
- [ ] Raheem Sterling

4 Who scored England's winning goal in the UEFA Women's EURO 2022 Championships?

- [ ] Beth Mead
- [ ] Alessia Russo
- [ ] Fran Kirby
- [ ] Chloe Kelly

5 Former Southampton striker Shane Long scored the fastest ever top-flight league goal in how many seconds?

- [ ] 7.69
- [ ] 24.64
- [ ] 2.10
- [ ] 132.31

6 Vivianne Miedema has achieved more hat-tricks than anyone else in top-flight English women's league history. How many has she scored?

- [ ] 7
- [ ] 13
- [ ] 5
- [ ] 28

7 When he played for Barcelona, for how many seasons was Lionel Messi top scorer in Spain?

- [ ] 17
- [ ] 10
- [ ] 8
- [ ] 2

8 In English top-flight history, which team has scored the most goals from inside the box?

- [ ] West Ham United
- [ ] Manchester United
- [ ] Southampton
- [ ] Manchester City

9 How many English top-flight league goals did Manchester City's Erling Haaland score in his first 19 matches?

- [ ] 11
- [ ] 34
- [ ] 7
- [ ] 25

10 Who was the youngest ever Manchester Utd player to score 15 goals in European competition?

- [ ] Scott McTominay
- [ ] Marcus Rashford
- [ ] Harry Maguire
- [ ] Anthony Martial

GOAL!

MIDFIELD GENERALS

FACT

At the base of every successful team is a player who can provide cover for their back four, as well as turn defence into attack in the blink of an eye. No one bosses the pitch like a holding midfielder!

FACT 1

CLOSING DOWN
A good defensive midfielder will always press opponents. This helps break up attacks and prevents them from building up pressure and possession.

FACT 2

FULL BLAST
A defensive midfielder needs to have energy to cover the whole pitch for 90 minutes. Between last-ditch tackles and lung-busting forward runs, they help the whole team operate.

PASSES
Whether they're playing it out from the back with intricate passing or launching precise long balls up the pitch, midfielders need to have a range of passes in their skill set.

FACT 3

DECLAN RICE
This energetic midfield boss is so important to West Ham's team that he has already made well over 200 appearances – and is the club captain!

WEST HAM UNITED

CASEMIRO
He often goes under the radar, but this matchday menace is a quality tackler who can sit deep with his defenders. His ability to read the game is the best in world football.

MANCHESTER UNITED

JOSHUA KIMMICH
Kimmich controls the midfield like he has eyes in the back of his head! He constantly checks his surroundings, so he can read the game and control the flow.

BAYERN MUNICH

FOOTY FORMATIONS

Draw pictures in the grids so that each column, row and box contains only one of each football symbol.

EASY

TOUGH

WORLD CLASS

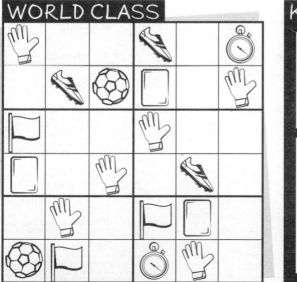

KEY

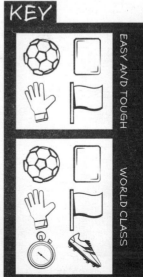

EASY AND TOUGH

WORLD CLASS

9

TRUE OR FALSE?

1 Liverpool's home kit was black and white until 1992.

TRUE ☐ FALSE ☐

2 The 2020 UEFA European Championships final, played in 2021, featured England and Italy.

TRUE ☐ FALSE ☐

3 There has never been an English league game on a Friday.

TRUE ☐ FALSE ☐

4 Harry Kane began his professional career as a centre-back.

TRUE ☐ FALSE ☐

5 Arsenal have won the UEFA Women's Champions League nine times.

TRUE ☐ FALSE ☐

6 Video Assistant Referee (VAR) was first used in the Premier League in 2019.

TRUE ☐ FALSE ☐

7 Manchester United was the first club to win the current English top-flight league three years in a row.

TRUE ☐ FALSE ☐

8 There must be at least three minutes of injury time in every professional game.

TRUE ☐ FALSE ☐

A-MAZE-BALLS

After training sessions there are balls left all over the practice pitches. Find your way through this footy maze to get to the changing rooms as quickly as possible!

START

FINISH

THE BEST CLUB NICKNAMES

Every club has a nickname that fans will chant and commentators will use. How many clubs can you match with their nicknames in the list below?

CLUB

EVERTON

LEICESTER CITY

BRIGHTON & HOVE ALBION

CRYSTAL PALACE

AFC BOURNEMOUTH

WEST HAM UTD

BRENTFORD

MANCHESTER UTD

NICKNAME

THE BEES

THE SEAGULLS

THE CHERRIES

THE HAMMERS

THE RED DEVILS

THE FOXES

THE TOFFEES

THE EAGLES

FAMOUS STADIUMS

DIFFICULTY:

Go around the grounds and try these tough teasers all about football's slickest stadiums. How many of the 10 questions can you answer correctly?

1 When was the first game played at Manchester United's Old Trafford?

- [ ] 1910
- [ ] 1940
- [ ] 1970
- [ ] 2010

2 Which European club plays home games at the Santiago Bernabéu Stadium?

- [ ] Ajax
- [ ] Real Madrid
- [ ] FC Porto
- [ ] Monaco

3 Where was the UEFA Euro 2020 final, which happened in 2021, played?

- [ ] Nou Camp
- [ ] Stadio Olimpico
- [ ] Celtic Park
- [ ] Wembley Stadium

4 Which European team has a famous stadium section called The Yellow Wall?

- [ ] Bayern Munich
- [ ] Lazio
- [ ] Marseille
- [ ] Borussia Dortmund

YELLOW

5 Which London club's stadium has the postcode SW6 6H?

- [ ] Fulham
- [ ] Chelsea
- [ ] Arsenal
- [ ] Queen's Park Rangers

6 Which of these stadiums has the highest capacity?

- [ ] Goodison Park
- [ ] King Power Stadium
- [ ] Carrow Road
- [ ] Vitality Stadium

7 Which of these stadiums has the lowest capacity?

- [ ] Villa Park
- [ ] Tottenham Hotspur Stadium
- [ ] St James' Park
- [ ] Molineux Stadium

8 Parc des Princes is home to which club?

- [ ] Lille OSC
- [ ] PSV Eindhoven
- [ ] Paris Saint-Germain
- [ ] Sporting Lisbon

9 The Mighty Red mascot is enjoyed by fans at which ground?

- [ ] Anfield
- [ ] London Stadium
- [ ] Stamford Bridge
- [ ] Elland Road

10 How tall is the famous arch over Wembley Stadium in London?

- [ ] 13 metres
- [ ] 103 metres
- [ ] 33 metres
- [ ] 133 metres

TOP TEN HUNT

DIFFICULTY:

Ten fantastic UEFA Champions League teams can be found in the grid. How long will it take you to spot them all?

N	Y	T	I	C	R	E	T	S	E	H	C	N	A	M
I	E	H	K	S	E	P	I	K	D	U	M	E	A	K
A	O	A	P	U	I	L	C	F	I	I	C	H	C	M
M	G	T	I	T	H	A	D	G	J	A	N	R	U	A
R	H	L	C	N	R	O	X	K	C	E	E	N	L	N
E	S	E	R	E	E	C	K	O	T	I	F	I	P	A
G	C	T	E	V	D	S	G	T	H	T	T	J	B	L
T	O	I	F	U	N	Q	O	K	X	E	O	L	C	I
N	R	C	G	J	A	T	I	A	C	F	I	R	E	M
I	B	O	H	K	M	I	J	B	D	G	J	B	C	C
A	U	M	I	A	R	B	A	R	C	E	L	O	N	A
S	B	A	Y	E	R	N	M	U	N	I	C	H	J	J
S	N	D	K	C	H	L	B	E	Y	A	B	A	H	I
I	Y	R	A	D	C	E	H	G	G	K	X	H	E	S
R	D	I	B	B	A	C	M	A	M	N	B	J	P	R
A	F	D	A	A	T	E	U	J	U	I	T	U	A	I
P	T	F	A	J	A	T	X	C	E	L	T	A	K	F

- ☐ Barcelona
- ☐ Juventus
- ☐ Paris Saint-Germain
- ☐ Manchester City
- ☐ Atlético Madrid
- ☐ Celtic
- ☐ Bayern Munich
- ☐ Ajax
- ☐ Tottenham
- ☐ AC Milan

IT TOOK ME ...

_____/_____
minutes / seconds

SAFE HANDS

As the last line of defence, a top-quality goalkeeper can be the difference between winning and losing trophies! Every world-class team needs a superstar stopper between the posts to record vital clean sheets.

THIBAUT COURTOIS

Courtois is the king keeper at Real Madrid! He dominates attackers, has the agility to make top reaction saves and can pick a perfect pass.

REAL MADRID

FACT 1

FLYING SAVES
As well as looking spectacular, pulling out impressive saves is key for a goalkeeper. The position requires great agility, reflexes and bravery. Saves save the day!

EDERSON

Ederson can do it all in goalkeeper gloves! His saves are extraordinary and he's rarely caught out of position. He's one of the very best at kicking and throwing to his teammates, too!

MANCHESTER CITY

FACT 2

COMMANDING AREA
A goalkeeper needs to boss their area. Opponents should know that if the play enters this space, he or she will attract the ball like a magnet!

AARON RAMSDALE

Arsenal's awesome no. 1 has risen from the lower leagues to prove he's a proper hero. Ramsdale is sharp in one-on-ones and works very well with his defenders!

ARSENAL

PASS MASTER
A modern goalkeeper must be great with their feet, too. Being able to accurately kick or throw the ball to a teammate can launch a quick counter-attack.

FACT 3

NAME GAME

Fill in the missing letters to complete this dream team.
If you can complete them all, put your name down as
their mega new manager!

ED _ _ S _ N
GK

WA _ _ E _   V _ N D _ J _   _ L A B _
RB   **CB**   **LB**

F _ D E _   _ _ U N T
CM   **CM**

B _ _ L I N _ H _ M   R A P _ _ N _ A
RW   **LW**

K _ N _   _ A A _ A _ D   M B _ _ _ É
RF   **CF**   **LF**

DREAM TEAM MANAGER'S NAME

_ _ _ _ _ _ _ _ _ _ _ _ _ _ _ _ _ _ _

KNOW YOUR STUFF

DIFFICULTY: ⚽ ⚽ ⚽

Use the clues below to work out the different footy terms or phrases to complete the crossword. Good luck getting them all to match up!

DOWN

1 When a team's forwards and midfielders put pressure on the opposition defenders and goalkeeper, they are playing a high ... (5)
2 A player on the touchline, ready to come on if needed in a game, is a what? (10)
3 The system and style a team plays could be called their ... (7)
4 This colour card is shown by a referee when a player is sent off (3)

ACROSS

5 This video system helps the referee make important decisions (3)
6 If a goalkeeper can't catch the ball, they may decide to do this instead (5)
7 The referee has at least two of these people to help control a game (9)
8 In North America and many other places, football is called this (6)

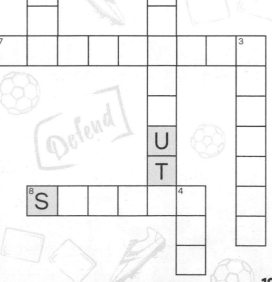

TOP DEFENDERS

DIFFICULTY: ⚽ ⚽ ⚽

Time to tackle ten quiz questions about awesome defenders! These players know how to stop goals going in, but will your answers be blocked as well?

1 Which of these defenders is the eldest?

☐ Kyle Walker ☐ Thiago Silva

☐ Eric Dier ☐ Ben White

2 Varane, Pavard, Kimpembe and Koundé have all played international football for which country?

☐ Netherlands ☐ Portugal

☐ Spain ☐ France

3 Reece James is a Chelsea and England star, but which team did he join on loan in 2018?

☐ Newcastle United ☐ Huddersfield Town

☐ Wigan Athletic ☐ Borussia Dortmund

4 Which defender won eight English league titles, all with the same club?

☐ John Terry ☐ Gary Neville

☐ Rio Ferdinand ☐ Vincent Kompany

5 In which year did centre-back legend Leah Williamson first play for the senior England team?

☐ 2020   ☐ 2022   ☐ 2018   ☐ 2015

6 Who made an impressive 104 tackles in the 2021-22 English top-flight season?

☐ Tyrick Mitchell   ☐ Adam Webster

☐ Joao Cancelo   ☐ Harry Maguire

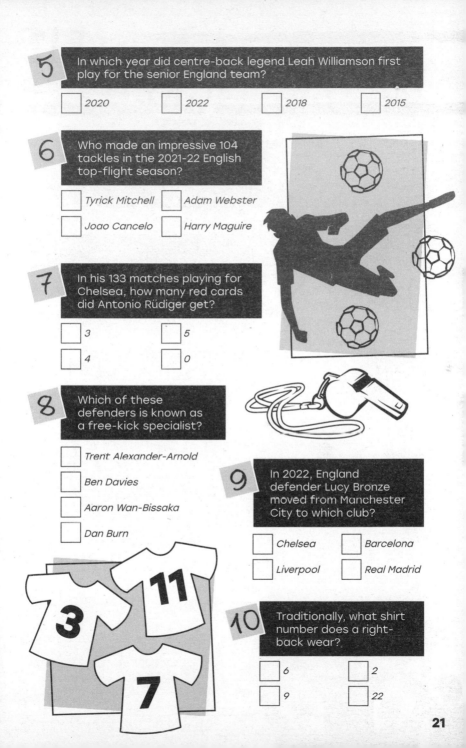

7 In his 133 matches playing for Chelsea, how many red cards did Antonio Rüdiger get?

☐ 3   ☐ 5

☐ 4   ☐ 0

8 Which of these defenders is known as a free-kick specialist?

☐ Trent Alexander-Arnold

☐ Ben Davies

☐ Aaron Wan-Bissaka

☐ Dan Burn

9 In 2022, England defender Lucy Bronze moved from Manchester City to which club?

☐ Chelsea   ☐ Barcelona

☐ Liverpool   ☐ Real Madrid

10 Traditionally, what shirt number does a right-back wear?

☐ 6   ☐ 2

☐ 9   ☐ 22

KIT DESIGN

A flashy and fashionable kit is an important part of the game. Design your own kit here and impress other footy fans with your slick style and winning colours!

ATTACKING MIDFIELDERS

Scoring and creating goals is what attacking midfielders are in the team for! They are creative, skilful and whenever they receive the ball, their aim is to get it up the pitch. Fans love what they bring to a match!

FACT 1

VERSATILE SKILLS
These attacking aces need strength to win and keep the ball, intelligence to pass precisely and good finishing to hit up to ten goals a season!

FACT 2

PARTNERSHIP
They require strong partnerships with key teammates. These include the main forward and usually a defensive midfielder, constantly giving and taking the ball to set up chances.

FACT 3

STEALTH STRIKE
Coaches love it when attacking midfielders deploy 'stealth mode', meaning they go undetected by opponents and then pop up with a crucial chance!

I'm invisible!

MASON MOUNT
Watch Double M for 90 minutes to see him glide through midfield, hover around the box and know exactly when to shoot or pass to a Chelsea pal!

CHELSEA

BRUNO FERNANDES
Fernandes is very tough to stop, and that's why he's brilliant for Manchester United. His movement, shooting, passing and set-piece skills are unbeatable!

MANCHESTER UNITED

BERNARDO SILVA
Silva can play in any attacking position for City, because he's so slick on the ball and can control the tempo of attack. Inside the box, his quick feet get results.

MANCHESTER CITY

TRUE OR FALSE?

1 The FIFA World Cup Trophy is over 200 years old.

TRUE ☐ FALSE ☐

2 The first men's FA Cup Final was in 1872.

TRUE ☐ FALSE ☐

3 The first women's FA Cup Final was in 1971.

TRUE ☐ FALSE ☐

4

England's Lionesses were champions of the world in 2015 and 2019.

TRUE ☐ FALSE ☐

5

The winners of the men's FA Cup earn a place in the UEFA Champions League.

TRUE ☐ FALSE ☐

6

Real Madrid and Atlético Madrid share the same stadium.

TRUE ☐ FALSE ☐

7

French club Paris Saint-Germain was founded in 1970.

TRUE ☐ FALSE ☐

8

Celtic was the first British team to win the European Cup (what the UEFA Champions League was originally called).

TRUE ☐ FALSE ☐

CLUBS

DIFFICULTY:

You might support one particular club, but to be a true footy fan, you need to know a bit about wider football history. If you do, you'll score well on these pages!

1 Which famous club is nicknamed The Magpies?

- [ ] West Ham United
- [ ] Newcastle United
- [ ] Sunderland
- [ ] Sheffield Wednesday

2 Which club used to be called Newton Heath?

- [ ] Bolton Wanderers
- [ ] Brentford
- [ ] Manchester United
- [ ] Cardiff City

3 Can you pick out the two clubs that share a stadium?

- [ ] Aston Villa & Birmingham
- [ ] Bristol City & Bristol Rovers
- [ ] AC Milan & Inter Milan
- [ ] Hearts & Hibernian

4 Which of these clubs does not have a home kit that is mostly blue?

- [ ] Rangers
- [ ] Ipswich Town
- [ ] Atlético Madrid
- [ ] Napoli

5 The famous names of Shankly, Dalglish, Rush and Fowler are all connected to which club?

☐ Barcelona ☐ Liverpool ☐ Juventus ☐ Manchester City

6 Which club did Frank Lampard play for and then later manage in his career?

☐ Chelsea ☐ Dundee United

☐ Tottenham Hostpur ☐ Southampton

7 If a supporter is called a 'Gooner', which club do they follow?

☐ Boca Juniors ☐ Arsenal

☐ Sheffield United ☐ Plymouth

8 Which club's badge features a white outline of a tree?

☐ Fulham

☐ Nottingham Forest

☐ Leicester City

☐ Brighton & Hove Albion

9 James Milner played his first professional game aged 16, but which club was it for?

☐ Leeds United

☐ Crystal Palace

☐ West Bromwich Albion

☐ Reading

10 Manchester City is a hugely successful club, but when did it first win the current top-flight league?

☐ 2001-02 ☐ 2011-12

☐ 2010-11 ☐ 2015-16

SUPER STRIKERS

FACT

Goals win games and they're mostly scored by strikers! Being a fearsome goal-getter requires power, ruthlessness, speed and a natural ability to find the net from the slightest chance. Goals are priceless, which is why strikers are expensive!

TOP TACTICS
Strikers do damage in the box, but they have to fit in with the team's tactics. This may mean pressing defenders, collecting long balls or beating the offside trap.

FACT 1

SHOOTING RANGE
An elite striker is never afraid to shoot. They are greedy, but have the confidence to know they can hit the target. Accurate heading and cool penalties will help, too!

FACT 2

FINDING SPACE
A centre-back will stay close to a striker to keep them quiet. Drifting into space and coming alive when the ball is put through gives the forward a surprise advantage!

FACT 3

KYLIAN MBAPPÉ

Simply one of the best strikers on the planet! He's blessed with mega speed, fab technique and an ability to play centrally and out wide!

PARIS SAINT-GERMAIN

ALESSIA RUSSO

Playing for England and Manchester United, Russo's powerful shots and ability to convert passes makes her a huge goal threat.

MANCHESTER UNITED

HARRY KANE

In March 2022, Kane scored his 300th career goal. The England star can play as a traditional no. 9 and lead the line, or drop deeper in a no. 10 role. Pure quality!

TOTTENHAM

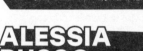

ROUTE TO THE FINAL

DIFFICULTY:

Can you spot the real football stadium names in each of the rows below? Only one is correct – the rest are all made up, but can you work out which?

1 GREEN PARK | THRILLER PARK | VILLA PARK | ASTON STADIUM

2 TURF MERE | STADIUM OF FRIGHT | RIVERSLIDE STADIUM | BRAMALL LANE

3 DEEPDALE | DEEPDOWN | DEEPGATE | DEEPGROUND

4 ST. STEVEN'S | ST. MARY'S | ST. LUKE'S | ST. KEVIN'S

5 BRICK STADIUM | BRONX STADIUM | IBROX STADIUM | BRILLIANT STADIUM

6 EMIRATES STADIUM | MIRAGE STADIUM | DREAM STADIUM | LIGHTNING STADIUM

ENGLISH LEAGUE

DIFFICULTY:

It's the most exciting domestic football league on the planet, packed with the biggest and best teams and players. Check out whether you're a top-flight pro!

1 Who won the first season of the current top-flight?

- [ ] Arsenal
- [ ] Man Utd
- [ ] Norwich
- [ ] Blackburn

2 By the end of the 2021-22 top-flight season, how many different clubs had won the current trophy?

- [ ] 4
- [ ] 6
- [ ] 7
- [ ] 9

3 Which one of these legends never played in the English top-flight?

- [ ] Zlatan Ibrahimovic
- [ ] Thierry Henry
- [ ] Kaká
- [ ] Didier Deschamps

4 Which team went unbeaten in the English top-flight 2003-04 season?

- [ ] Manchester United
- [ ] Blackburn Rovers
- [ ] Tottenham Hotspur
- [ ] Arsenal

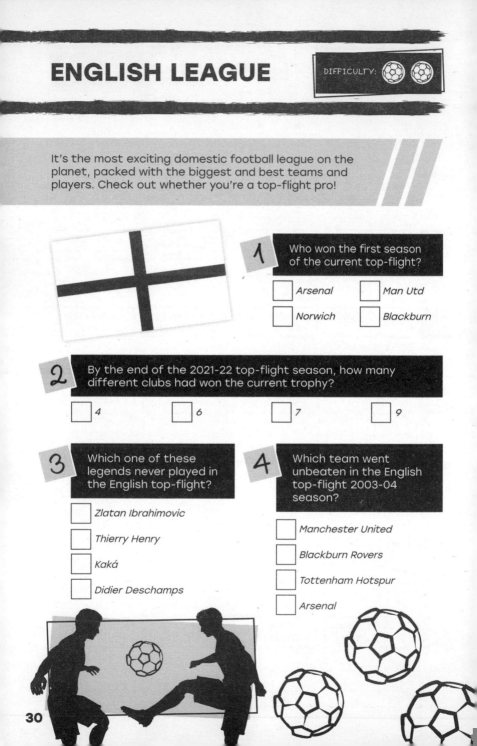

5 How many league games does each top-flight team play in a season?

☐ 40 ☐ 36

☐ 38 ☐ 19

6 How tall is the English top-flight trophy?

☐ 44cm ☐ 84cm

☐ 64cm ☐ 104cm

7 Derby County set a record for fewest points won in a season in 2007-08. How many was it?

☐ 0 points ☐ 18 points

☐ 11 points ☐ 28 points

8 Which club was the first to reach 100 points in a single top-flight season?

☐ Manchester City

☐ Chelsea

☐ Leicester City

☐ Liverpool

9 In the 1992-93 season, Wimbledon v. Everton became famous for which of these reasons?

☐ 113 goals ☐ Lowest attendance

☐ 13 debuts ☐ A dog was in goal

10 Tottenham Hotspur v. Arsenal in 2017-18, played at Wembley Stadium, set the highest top-flight league attendance. What was it?

☐ 63,222 ☐ 83,222

☐ 73,222 ☐ 103,222

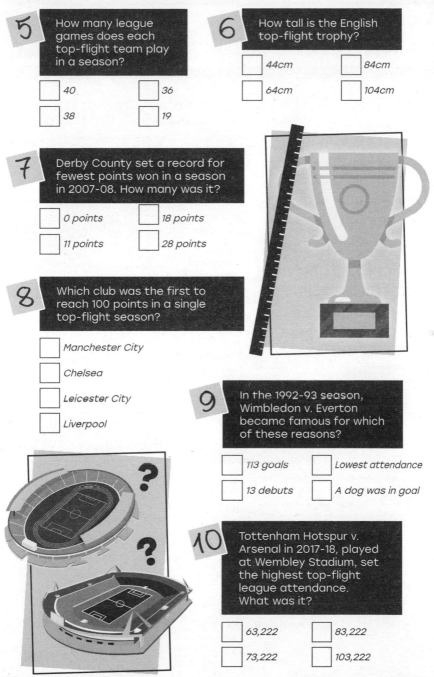

NUMBER KNOWLEDGE

Each of these groups of players are connected because they wear the same shirt number in club football. Just write the correct number by each list.

GROUP 1

KANE

NEYMAR

RASHFORD

MODRIC

_ _ _ _ _

GROUP 2

DEMBÉLÉ

MILNER

SON

SAKA

_ _ _ _ _

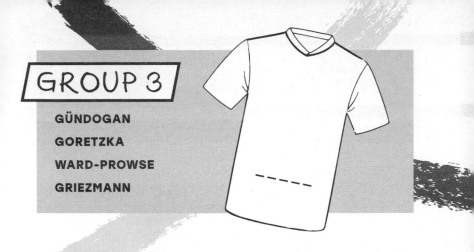

GROUP 3

GÜNDOGAN
GORETZKA
WARD-PROWSE
GRIEZMANN

GROUP 4

PICKFORD
ALISSON
ARRIZABALAGA
MARTINEZ

GROUP 5

RICHARLISON
MARTIAL
HAALAND
HALLER

THE BOSS

The 11 players on the pitch do their best to get a win. Off the pitch, the manager must decide on lots of things – tactics, formations, which players to start, when to make subs and much more. Being 'the boss' isn't easy!

FACT 1

TRAINING TIME

On non-matchdays, players go to training. Here, a manager works to improve the squad, make them fitter and school them in tactics and style.

FACT 2

DIFFICULT DECISIONS

With a whole squad to choose from, a manager must make tough choices. Which strikers are on form? Is the goalkeeper playing well? Will a winger make an impact? The boss has a lot to decide!

TRANSFER CHOICES

A manager has a big say in which players the club buys and sells. Buying a new striker can be the difference between a club staying up or being relegated!

FACT 3

SARINA WIEGMAN

Wiegman coached the England women's team to success at UEFA Euro 2022. She likes a settled team in a 4-3-3 system with versatile forwards.

ENGLAND WOMEN

CARLO ANCELOTTI

This Italian manager is one of the most experienced in the game. In 2022, he won his fourth UEFA Champions League, with Real Madrid.

REAL MADRID

JÜRGEN KLOPP

Klopp has transformed Liverpool since 2015. He has won the UEFA Champions League and league titles thanks to a pressing, attacking style and clever recruitment!

LIVERPOOL

CODE BREAKER

The coach has scribbled a secret message to their team. Using the code-breaking instructions in the box below, work out what the message is!

16 1 19 19 **20 15** **20 8 5**
23 9 14 7 5 18 19 **13 15 18 5**

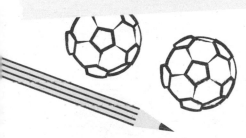

CODE BREAKING RULES

Each number represents where the letter comes in the alphabet. For example, 1 is A, 18 is R and 26 is Z.

THE CODED MESSAGE IS:

_ _ _ _   _ _   _ _ _

_ _ _ _ _ _ _   _ _ _ _

TRUE OR FALSE?

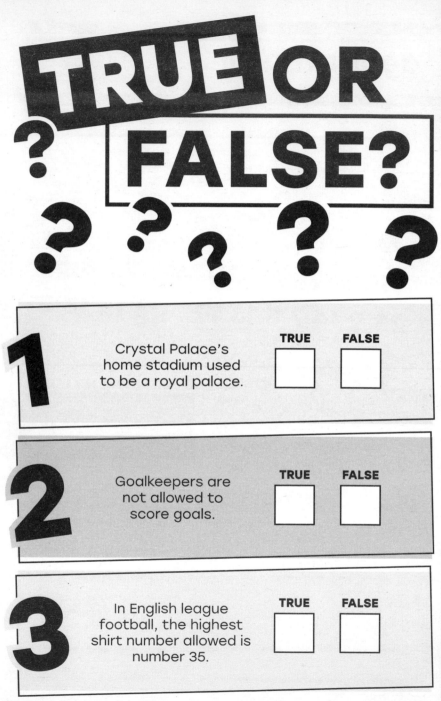

1

Crystal Palace's home stadium used to be a royal palace.

TRUE ☐ FALSE ☐

2

Goalkeepers are not allowed to score goals.

TRUE ☐ FALSE ☐

3

In English league football, the highest shirt number allowed is number 35.

TRUE ☐ FALSE ☐

4 Cristiano Ronaldo first signed for Manchester United in 2003.

TRUE ☐ FALSE ☐

5 Kevin De Bruyne played youth international football for England.

TRUE ☐ FALSE ☐

6 Jamie Vardy has scored more than 100 top-flight goals.

TRUE ☐ FALSE ☐

7 On the opening day of the 2022-23 season, a total of zero goals were scored.

TRUE ☐ FALSE ☐

8 Mohamed Salah began his English football career with Chelsea.

TRUE ☐ FALSE ☐

SPANISH LEAGUE

DIFFICULTY: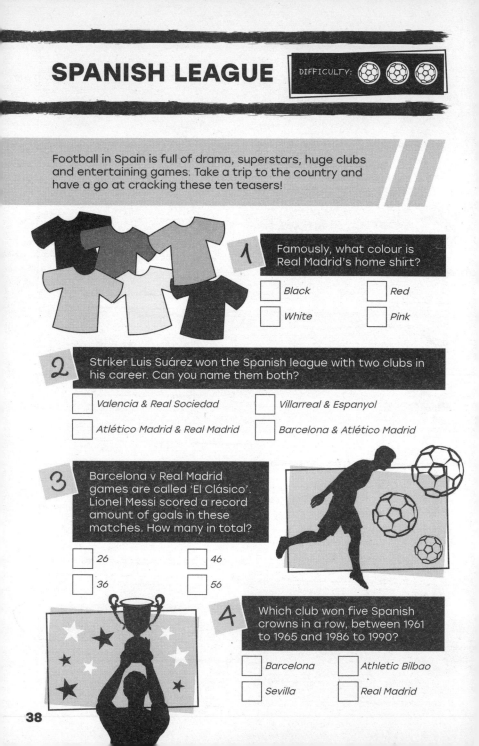

Football in Spain is full of drama, superstars, huge clubs and entertaining games. Take a trip to the country and have a go at cracking these ten teasers!

1 Famously, what colour is Real Madrid's home shirt?

- [ ] Black
- [ ] White
- [ ] Red
- [ ] Pink

2 Striker Luis Suárez won the Spanish league with two clubs in his career. Can you name them both?

- [ ] Valencia & Real Sociedad
- [ ] Atlético Madrid & Real Madrid
- [ ] Villarreal & Espanyol
- [ ] Barcelona & Atlético Madrid

3 Barcelona v Real Madrid games are called 'El Clásico'. Lionel Messi scored a record amount of goals in these matches. How many in total?

- [ ] 26
- [ ] 36
- [ ] 46
- [ ] 56

4 Which club won five Spanish crowns in a row, between 1961 to 1965 and 1986 to 1990?

- [ ] Barcelona
- [ ] Sevilla
- [ ] Athletic Bilbao
- [ ] Real Madrid

5 Can you name the club that plays their home games at the Benito Villamarin Stadium?

☐ Real Betis ☐ Valencia

☐ Mallorca ☐ Osasuna

6 Which one of these is not a Spanish club?

☐ Girona ☐ Celta Vigo

☐ Rayo Vallecano ☐ Braga

7 How many league goals did Cristiano Ronaldo score for Real Madrid between 2009 to 2018?

☐ 112 ☐ 412

☐ 312 ☐ 612

8 In which year did the top-flight Spanish league begin?

☐ 1889 ☐ 1939

☐ 1929 ☐ 1959

9 Who was the Spanish league's top scorer in the 2021-22 season?

☐ Vinícius Júnior ☐ Robert Lewandowski

☐ Iago Aspas ☐ Karim Benzema

10 Ousmane Dembele, Eden Hazard and Joao Felix all wore which number when playing in Spain in 2021-22?

☐ 10 ☐ 11

☐ 9 ☐ 7

SCRAMBLED STRIKERS

Can you rearrange these scrambled striker names to reveal all of the English top-flight league strikers listed below?

1 SESUJ

_ _ _ _ _

2 HALAS

_ _ _ _ _

3 MITRĆIVO

_ _ _ _ _ _ _ _

4 NOTEY

_ _ _ _ _

5 DARVY

_ _ _ _ _

6 RINGLEST

_ _ _ _ _ _ _ _

7 IKAS

_ _ _ _

8 FIROMIN

_ _ _ _ _ _ _

9 TONIOAN

_ _ _ _ _ _ _

10 WEBLECK

_ _ _ _ _ _ _

SLICK SKIPPERS

FACT

Every team has a captain to lead them through each match. The player wearing the armband has a duty to communicate with their players, plus the opposing team's captain and the match officials. Maximum respect!

FACT 1

TEAM TALK
Most captains are good communicators, supportive and ready to encourage the team. The skipper will often step forward and inspire their teammates!

GO TEAM!

FACT 2

REFEREE RESPECT
The referee may want to speak to captains if there's a problem during a match. The referee knows that if the captain is given an instruction, it will be shared with the whole team.

FACT 3

CLUB DUTY
Some teams have a club captain as well as an on-pitch captain. The club captain is an older player who doesn't always play, but is a leader in the changing room.

SERGIO BUSQUETS

As captain of Barcelona and Spain, two teams packed with superstars, Busquets is a calming influence from the middle of the pitch.

BARCELONA

MANUEL NEUER

Having a goalkeeper as captain is not always something managers like, but Neuer is a powerful character with a vast stack of trophies and leadership qualities.

BAYERN MUNICH

JAMES WARD -PROWSE

Ward-Prowse leads by example on the pitch. With his class, energy and midfield scheming – plus a few great free kicks and penalties – he is respected by his team.

SOUTHAMPTON

ENGLISH WOMEN'S LEAGUE

DIFFICULTY:

The top-flight English women's league is enjoying a rocket-powered rise thanks to amazing clubs, world-class players and huge attendances!

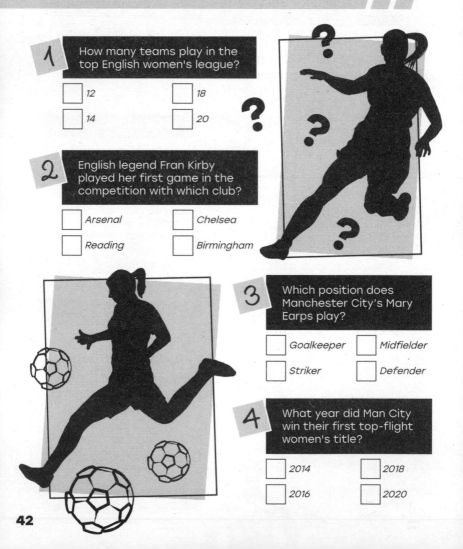

1 How many teams play in the top English women's league?

- [ ] 12
- [ ] 14
- [ ] 18
- [ ] 20

2 English legend Fran Kirby played her first game in the competition with which club?

- [ ] Arsenal
- [ ] Reading
- [ ] Chelsea
- [ ] Birmingham

3 Which position does Manchester City's Mary Earps play?

- [ ] Goalkeeper
- [ ] Striker
- [ ] Midfielder
- [ ] Defender

4 What year did Man City win their first top-flight women's title?

- [ ] 2014
- [ ] 2016
- [ ] 2018
- [ ] 2020

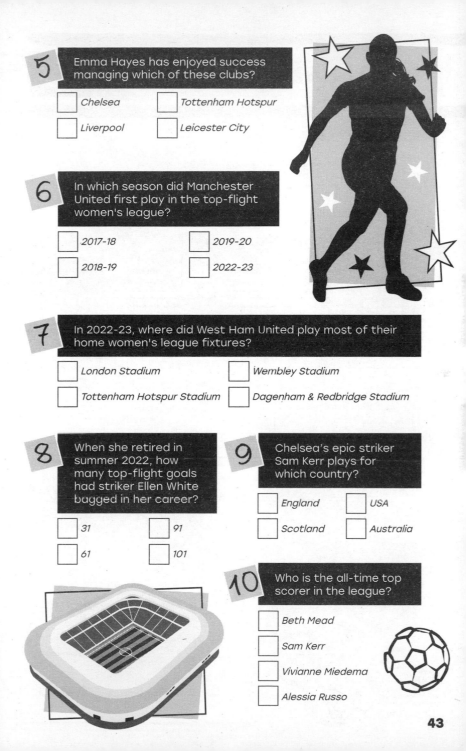

5 Emma Hayes has enjoyed success managing which of these clubs?

☐ Chelsea
☐ Tottenham Hotspur
☐ Liverpool
☐ Leicester City

6 In which season did Manchester United first play in the top-flight women's league?

☐ 2017-18
☐ 2019-20
☐ 2018-19
☐ 2022-23

7 In 2022-23, where did West Ham United play most of their home women's league fixtures?

☐ London Stadium
☐ Wembley Stadium
☐ Tottenham Hotspur Stadium
☐ Dagenham & Redbridge Stadium

8 When she retired in summer 2022, how many top-flight goals had striker Ellen White bagged in her career?

☐ 31
☐ 91
☐ 61
☐ 101

9 Chelsea's epic striker Sam Kerr plays for which country?

☐ England
☐ USA
☐ Scotland
☐ Australia

10 Who is the all-time top scorer in the league?

☐ Beth Mead
☐ Sam Kerr
☐ Vivianne Miedema
☐ Alessia Russo

MULTI BALL

This is a goalkeeper's nightmare! How many footballs are flying around here? Try to count them all and write your answer in the box.

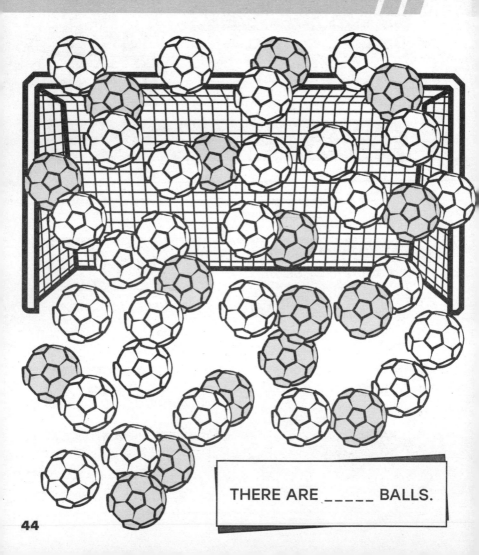

THERE ARE _ _ _ _ _ BALLS.

LEGEND LINES

These English league legends were a huge hit with their beloved clubs, but can you link them correctly? Draw a line between the legend and the team they played for.

LEGENDS

SERGIO AGÜERO

THIERRY HENRY

ALAN SHEARER

KASPER SCHMEICHEL

JAN VERTONGHEN

CRISTIANO RONALDO

SADIO MANÉ

JOHN TERRY

CLUBS

CHELSEA

TOTTENHAM

NEWCASTLE

ARSENAL

MANCHESTER UNITED

LIVERPOOL

LEICESTER CITY

MANCHESTER CITY

FRENCH LEAGUE

Fancy a contest about France's top-flight league? It is home to amazing players and powerful clubs, so see how you score. Bonne chance – that's 'good luck' in French!

1 How many goals did Kylian Mbappé score in the 2021-22 season?

- [ ] 19
- [ ] 35
- [ ] 28
- [ ] 40

2 How old was Lionel Messi when he joined Paris Saint-Germain in 2021?

- [ ] 30
- [ ] 34
- [ ] 32
- [ ] 36

3 Which one of these clubs has never won the French championship?

- [ ] Troyes
- [ ] Saint-Étienne
- [ ] Lyon
- [ ] Bordeaux

4 What is Mauricio Pochettino's connection to French giants Paris Saint-Germain (PSG)?

- [ ] He has only played for PSG
- [ ] He has only managed PSG
- [ ] He has played for and managed PSG
- [ ] He owns PSG

5 Which of these teams doesn't compete in France's top league?

☐ Stade Rennais ☐ Lorient

☐ Lens ☐ Club Brugge

6 Montpellier goalkeeper Jonas Omlin made the most saves in the 2021-22 season. How many was it?

☐ 40 ☐ 80 ☐ 120 ☐ 1,200

7 Which of these legends never played in France?

☐ David Beckham

☐ Ronaldinho

☐ Karim Benzema

☐ Sergio Agüero

8 How many teams were relegated from France's top-flight league at the end of 2022-23?

☐ 4 ☐ 2

☐ 3 ☐ 0

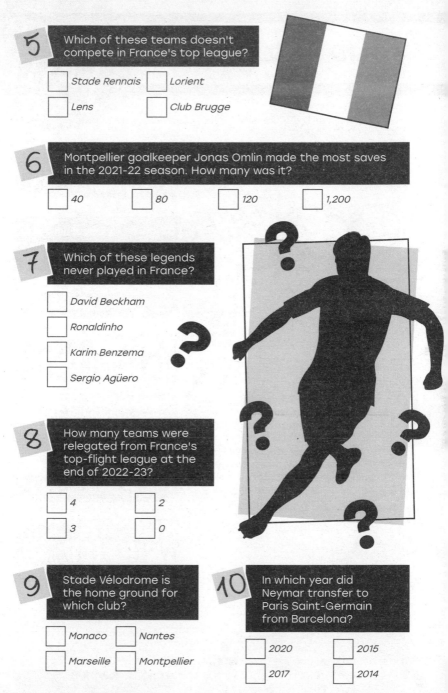

9 Stade Vélodrome is the home ground for which club?

☐ Monaco ☐ Nantes

☐ Marseille ☐ Montpellier

10 In which year did Neymar transfer to Paris Saint-Germain from Barcelona?

☐ 2020 ☐ 2015

☐ 2017 ☐ 2014

SOLID DEFENCE

FACT

A team may score goals with ease, but if it can't defend properly, then that's a big problem. Defenders organise the back line and when a team is set up in a defensive style, the whole team has to help out!

FACT 1

KEEP OUT
Defenders want the ball to be away from their own goal. This can be done by winning tackles and clearing, but many teams play a passing game from the back!

FACT 2

MIX IT UP
In a defensive unit, it's great to have a mix of skills. A tall and strong centre-back playing with a speedier partner is ideal, and if the full-backs can attack and defend, they can deal with anything!

FACT 3

DEFENSIVE STYLE
Defenders must be able to adapt to different formations and even switch styles during a game. For example, you can have a back two, or a back three!

ANTONIO RÜDIGER

Why did Real Madrid bring Rüdiger to the club in 2022 from Chelsea? Because he is a tough tackling defender that bosses the back line.

REAL MADRID

VIRGIL VAN DIJK

Liverpool's success has been built on a few key players, and one of those is centre-back van Dijk. He makes defending look easy and graceful.

LIVERPOOL

KIERAN TRIPPIER

Trippier is at home playing right-back, but he's so skilful he can also fill in on the other flank. He is super solid, tackles very well and offers loads going forward!

NEWCASTLE

MATCH ATTAX MIX

DIFFICULTY:

A Match Attax card has been divided into five strips. Your task is to put the card back together. Can you work out what order the card needs to go in?

GERMAN LEAGUE

DIFFICULTY:

Have you seen Germany's top-flight league in action?
It's awesome to watch, with talented stars on the pitch
and super-passionate fans packing the stadiums!

1 Bayern Munich were top-flight
champions in 2021-22. How many
titles was this in a row for the club?

☐ 5

☐ 10

☐ 15

☐ 20

2 Manager Pep Guardiola won three
German titles with which club?

☐ Borussia Dortmund

☐ Mainz 05

☐ Bayer Leverkusen

☐ Bayern Munich

3 When he played in Germany, how
many top-flight goals did Robert
Lewandowski smash in?

☐ 234

☐ 312

☐ 411

☐ 656

21

4 What shirt number does Sadio
Mané wear for German giants
Bayern Munich?

☐ 8

☐ 10

☐ 30

☐ 17

5 In which year did the current top league's first games kick-off?

☐ 1903
☐ 1943
☐ 1963
☐ 2003

1973

6 Jude Bellingham, Jadon Sancho and Marco Reus all played for which team?

☐ Schalke 04
☐ Borussia Dortmund
☐ Stuttgart
☐ Werder Bremen

7 What usually happens in the German league about halfway through the season?

☐ League-wide Christmas party
☐ Penalty shoot-out competition
☐ Referees go on holiday
☐ Winter break

8 Which one of these English league stars has not played in the German top-flight?

☐ Heung-min Son
☐ Bruno Fernandes
☐ Christian Pulisic
☐ Pierre-Emerick Aubameyang

9 When did legendary striker Thomas Müller score his first German top-flight goal?

☐ 2003
☐ 2009
☐ 2015
☐ 2019

10 Which famous manager has not won the German top-flight title?

☐ Pep Guardiola
☐ Louis van Gaal
☐ Felix Magath
☐ Graham Potter

MAZY RUN

Can you work out which of these mazy runs leads all the way to the goal? Like a defender trying to track a speedy forward, you'll need to pay close attention!

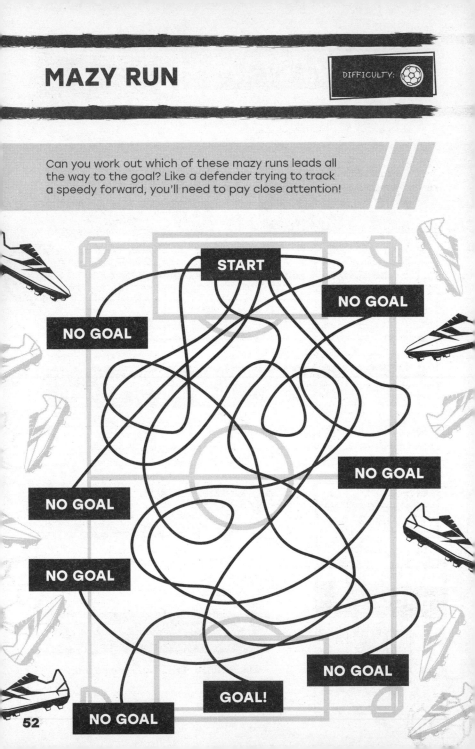

START

NO GOAL

NO GOAL

NO GOAL

NO GOAL

NO GOAL

NO GOAL

GOAL!

NO GOAL

DIFFICULTY:

Hidden inside this wordsearch are ten superstars of women's football. Scan the grid carefully to pick them all out. Write down how long it took you to spot the lot!

P	G	P	C	R	M	Z	Q	N	K
D	L	E	U	K	I	X	J	I	M
G	U	H	N	T	N	E	R	A	I
R	F	S	Z	G	E	B	W	U	M
E	X	Q	K	W	Y	L	V	N	E
B	R	O	N	Z	E	R	L	T	A
R	R	M	P	P	O	P	B	A	D
E	E	D	C	M	B	I	N	R	S
G	C	M	I	E	D	E	M	A	Y
E	R	E	N	A	R	D	Q	Z	J
H	W	H	A	U	A	T	R	A	M

HEGERBERG

MEAD

BRONZE

MARTA

RENARD

POPP

MIEDEMA

PUTELLAS

KIRBY

WEIR

IT TOOK ME...

☐ UNDER 2 MINUTES ☐ 2-3 MINUTES

☐ 3-4 MINUTES ☐ 4+ MINUTES

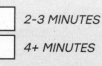

TRUE OR FALSE?

???????

1
Every English football season begins on 1 August.

TRUE ☐   FALSE ☐

2
Senegal star Sadio Mané used to play for Southampton.

TRUE ☐   FALSE ☐

3
The Tottenham Hotspur Stadium has a capacity of 80,000.

TRUE ☐   FALSE ☐

4 Only players aged 21 or under can join an English club on loan.

TRUE ☐ FALSE ☐

5 The most points an English team can win in one single season is 114.

TRUE ☐ FALSE ☐

6 Only a team's captain is allowed to talk to the referee during a game.

TRUE ☐ FALSE ☐

7 Pierre-Emerick Aubameyang has played for Chelsea, Arsenal and Tottenham.

TRUE ☐ FALSE ☐

8 Games between Barcelona and Real Madrid are known as 'El Clásico'.

TRUE ☐ FALSE ☐

NEXT GEN STARS

FACT

With a new generation of talent ready to burst through and make a big mark in the leagues, the UEFA Champions League and on the international stage, the future of football looks exciting! Check them out!

STEADY PROGRESS

Most teenagers that break through to the first team still need time to develop, meaning they will not play every game. Playing too often can cause lots of pressure.

FACT 1

LOAN MOVE

Many young players enjoy a loan spell away from their club. This gives them the chance to play regularly at a good level. Chelsea's Conor Gallagher had a few loan spells that really boosted his career.

FACT 2

TROPHY TASTE

Winning trophies at youth level is a great way to build a teenager's career. Manchester City's Phil Foden won an under-17 tournament with England in 2017!

FACT 3

ETHAN NWANERI

Nwaneri made his debut in 2022, aged 15, and became the English top-flight league's youngest ever player! He has a big future ahead of him.

ARSENAL

GAVI

Look out for all-action midfielder Gavi leading Barcelona and Spain to trophies! Before the age of 19, he became one of the first names on the team sheet, thanks to his skill and composure.

BARCELONA

IKER BRAVO

Born in 2005, the tall forward spent time with Leverkusen in Germany in 2021-22, but he's hoping to make an impact on loan in Spain. Bravo has every chance of breaking through soon.

BAYER LEVERKUSEN

MYSTERY STARS

These shady stars are keeping their identity in the dark!
Check out the clues for each player and have a go at
guessing who they really are.

PLAYER 1

I play for Manchester City! I
scored England's winner in the
UEFA Women's Euro 2022 final.

I think it's
_____

PLAYER 2

I am an assist star.
I have many English top-flight
titles. My initials are KDB.

I think it's
_____

PLAYER 3

I've played for two London
clubs. I had a brief spell with
Barcelona in 2022. I'm a
creative forward.

I think it's
_____

PLAYER 4

Am I the greatest of all time?
I'm a Spanish league legend
with an epic left foot.

I think it's
_____

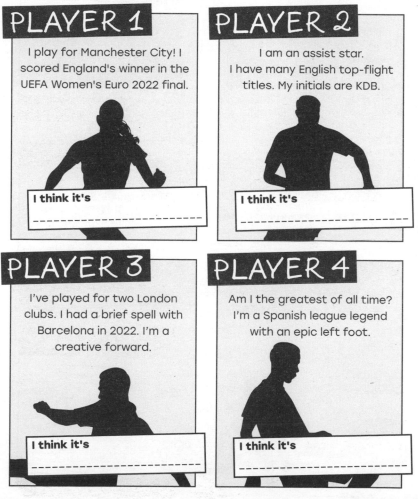

UEFA CHAMPIONS LEAGUE

DIFFICULTY:

It's the ultimate club competition on the planet that all the top teams chase. Have a go at these ten tricky UEFA Champions League questions!

1 How many UEFA Champions League goals did Ronaldo score for Real Madrid?

☐ 15
☐ 25
☐ 55
☐ 105

2 In 2021-22, Lyon won the UEFA Women's Champions League. How many wins were needed?

☐ 11
☐ 2
☐ 4
☐ 14

3 Which of these teams has never won the men's UEFA Champions League?

☐ Bayern Munich
☐ Inter Milan
☐ Arsenal
☐ Borussia Dortmund

4 Wing wizard Ángel Di María first played in the UEFA Champions League with which team?

☐ Benfica
☐ Manchester United
☐ Paris Saint-Germain
☐ Juventus

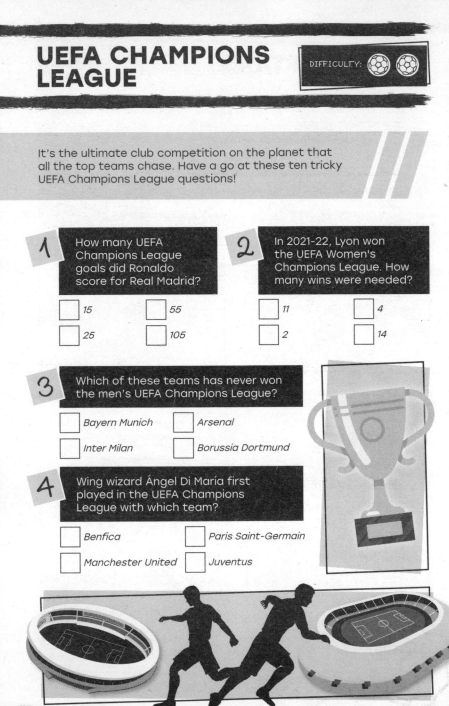

5 In 2021-22, a record UEFA Women's Champions League crowd watched Barcelona v Wolfsburg. How big was it?

- [ ] 21,648
- [ ] 51,648
- [ ] 91,648
- [ ] 101,648

6 Who once said that the famous UEFA Champions League theme was their alarm tone?

- [ ] Erling Haaland
- [ ] Romelu Lukaku
- [ ] Lucy Bronze
- [ ] Lionel Messi

7 Jose Mourinho first won the UEFA Champions League as the manager of which club?

- [ ] Real Madrid
- [ ] Chelsea
- [ ] Manchester United
- [ ] Porto

8 Which team played in the UEFA Champions League final in 2022, 2019, 2018, 2007 and 2005?

- [ ] Liverpool
- [ ] Manchester City
- [ ] Monaco
- [ ] Tottenham

9 What was unusual about the 2020 UEFA Champions League final?

- [ ] It kicked off at midday
- [ ] It was played in August
- [ ] It was over two legs
- [ ] 12 goals were scored

10 Traditionally, in which month does the UEFA Champions League group stage begin?

- [ ] June
- [ ] September
- [ ] May
- [ ] December

PINPOINT PASSERS

DIFFICULTY: ⚽⚽

Can you be as accurate with your answers as these stars are with their passing? Read the clues, then fill in each name to complete this crossword of perfect passers!

ACROSS

6 Experienced Liverpool and England leader (9)
7 Chelsea's assist (and penalty) master (8)
8 Started with Villa, now a City title winner (8)

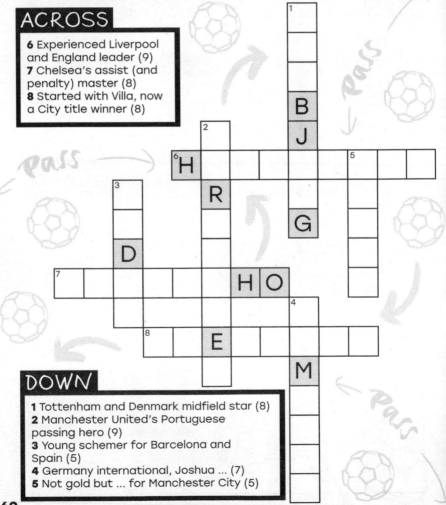

DOWN

1 Tottenham and Denmark midfield star (8)
2 Manchester United's Portuguese passing hero (9)
3 Young schemer for Barcelona and Spain (5)
4 Germany international, Joshua ... (7)
5 Not gold but ... for Manchester City (5)

GOALIE GRIDS

DIFFICULTY:

Another sudoku test! Draw pictures in the grids so that each column, row and box contains only one of each symbol.

EASY

TOUGH

WORLD CLASS

KEY
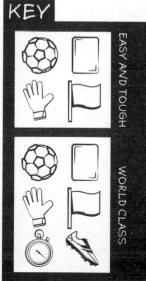

EASY AND TOUGH

WORLD CLASS

WOMEN'S LEAGUE

FACT

Top-flight women's football in England has seen massive growth, with even more pro teams and world-class talent. It started in 2011 and has grown massively – every matchday is full of great goals!

FACT 1

NEW ARRIVALS
The women's top-flight league has seen big clubs battling for top spot! Manchester United and Tottenham entered in 2019, and their matches are so exciting!

FACT 2

PRESSURE PLAY
The spotlight has been on women's football recently, with record attendances and big transfers. Top players have to deal with the pressure and keep focused on the pitch to deliver success!

GOAL GLORY
The race to win the top-scorer award each season is electric. Strikers such as Vivianne Miedema and Sam Kerr have had to be on top form to claim the prize!

FACT 3

BETH MEAD

Beth Mead is a dangerous attacking talent for top team Arsenal. The England hero can play on either wing and loves to dribble into the box to blast a shot or assist!

ARSENAL

SAM KERR

Kerr claimed her third league title in 2022. The awesome Australian forward has been a constant goal machine for Chelsea and uses her movement, speed and finishing to boss the box!

CHELSEA

ELLA TOONE

A legendary England goalscorer, Toone's been firing in the goals and assists for club and country. She is brave in possession and works defenders tirelessly with her forward runs.

MANCHESTER UNITED

BOOT-IFUL PATH

What a nightmare – these boot laces are in a complete mess! Only one of them is connected to the footy boots. Can you work out which lace it is?

CAPTAINS

DIFFICULTY:

Whoever wears the captain's armband is the leader of the team. They can play in any position, but they are vital for their club. Test your captain knowledge now!

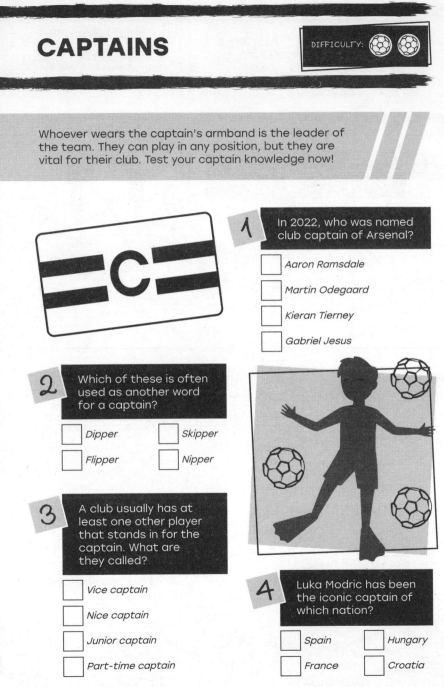

1 In 2022, who was named club captain of Arsenal?

- [ ] Aaron Ramsdale
- [ ] Martin Odegaard
- [ ] Kieran Tierney
- [ ] Gabriel Jesus

2 Which of these is often used as another word for a captain?

- [ ] Dipper
- [ ] Skipper
- [ ] Flipper
- [ ] Nipper

3 A club usually has at least one other player that stands in for the captain. What are they called?

- [ ] Vice captain
- [ ] Nice captain
- [ ] Junior captain
- [ ] Part-time captain

4 Luka Modric has been the iconic captain of which nation?

- [ ] Spain
- [ ] Hungary
- [ ] France
- [ ] Croatia

5 Which position does Chelsea women's captain Magdalena Eriksson play?

- [ ] Defender
- [ ] Winger
- [ ] Goalkeeper
- [ ] Striker

6 Who captained Manchester City to the Premier League title in the 2021-22 season?

- [ ] David Silva
- [ ] John Stones
- [ ] Sergio Aguero
- [ ] Fernandinho

CAPTAIN

7 Which of these clubs did Gareth Southgate not captain as a player?

- [ ] Tottenham Hotspur
- [ ] Crystal Palace
- [ ] Aston Villa
- [ ] Middlesbrough

8 Who captained France to world glory in 2018?

- [ ] Hugo Lloris
- [ ] Antoine Griezmann
- [ ] Paul Pogba
- [ ] N'Golo Kante

9 Together with the match officials, what do the captains do before the start of a game?

- [ ] Have a cup of tea
- [ ] Flip a coin
- [ ] Practise shooting
- [ ] Predict what the score will be

10 In which year did Cristiano Ronaldo first captain the senior Portugal football team?

- [ ] 2003
- [ ] 2010
- [ ] 2007
- [ ] 2015

STAT CAN'T BE RIGHT!

Each of these football cards includes wicked stats, but one of them is false. Can you circle the piece of incorrect info on each one?

ERIC DIER

Team:
Tottenham
Position:
Defender/midfielder
Top-flight debut:
2014
Born:
1994
Country:
Scotland

DECLAN RICE

Team:
West Ham
Position:
Defensive midfielder
Top-flight debut:
2020
Born:
1999
Country:
England

ÉDOUARD MENDY

Team:
Arsenal
Position:
Goalkeeper
Top-flight debut:
2020
Born:
1992
Country:
Senegal

CHRISTIAN ERIKSEN

Team:
Manchester United
Position:
Midfielder
Top-flight debut:
2013
Born:
2002
Country:
Denmark

BRUNO GUIMARÃES

Team:
Aston Villa
Position:
Midfielder
Top-flight debut:
2022
Born:
1997
Country:
Brazil

JAMES WARD-PROWSE

Team:
Southampton
Position:
Defender
Top-flight debut:
2012
Born: 1994
Country:
England

TROPHIES

Getting their hands on a shining trophy is the dream of every footballer! Now you can join in the trophy hunt, by seeing what you score with these ten questions.

1 Just before the English top-flight season starts, what's the name of the trophy that's usually played for at Wembley?

- [ ] Wembley Cup
- [ ] Community Shield
- [ ] Premier Cup
- [ ] Silver Shield

2 What's traditionally attached to a trophy, in the colours of the team that has just won it?

- [ ] Ribbons
- [ ] Stars
- [ ] Balloons
- [ ] Emojis

3 In another tradition, who usually lifts a trophy first when the team celebrates winning it?

- [ ] Manager
- [ ] Goalkeeper
- [ ] Goalscorer
- [ ] Captain

4 What round of a cup comes before the exciting semi-finals?

- [ ] Quarter finals
- [ ] Playoff finals
- [ ] Group finals
- [ ] First round

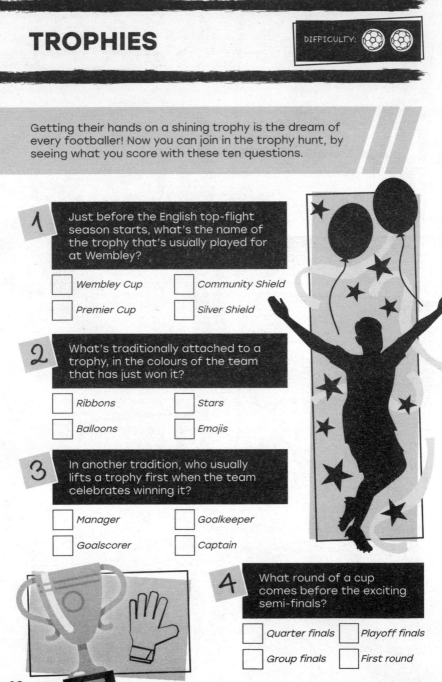

5 When England won the UEFA Women's Euro 2022 trophy, who did they beat in the final?

☐ Netherlands   ☐ France   ☐ USA   ☐ Germany

6 If a team wins three trophies in one season, what is it known as?

☐ A double   ☐ A quadruple

☐ A treble   ☐ An impossible

7 Which year was the UK's oldest cup founded?

☐ 1871   ☐ 2002

☐ 1877   ☐ 1954

8 In which season did Manchester City win domestic football's treble?

☐ 2011-12

☐ 2021-22

☐ 2018-19

☐ 2016-15

9 If a player wins a trophy, sometimes this is called winning a piece of what?

☐ Jewellery   ☐ Gold

☐ Silverware   ☐ Cake

10 During the trophy presentation after a final, what are both sets of players also usually awarded?

☐ A voucher   ☐ A medal

☐ A badge   ☐ Some boots

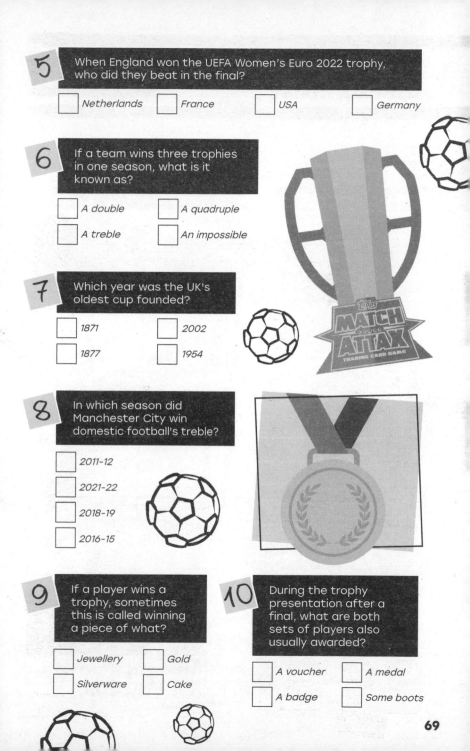

SPOT THE DIFFERENCE

You may have sharp skills on the pitch, but how sharp are you when it comes to a spot the difference test? Find and circle all eight changes when you spot them!

Colour in a football when you find each difference

TROPHY WINNERS

DIFFICULTY: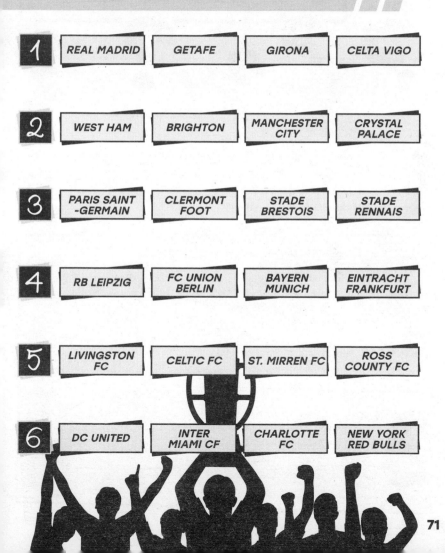

Starting at round one, work out your route to the trophy by selecting the real top-flight champion team's name in each row. Only one is correct – the rest have never won it.

1 REAL MADRID | GETAFE | GIRONA | CELTA VIGO

2 WEST HAM | BRIGHTON | MANCHESTER CITY | CRYSTAL PALACE

3 PARIS SAINT-GERMAIN | CLERMONT FOOT | STADE BRESTOIS | STADE RENNAIS

4 RB LEIPZIG | FC UNION BERLIN | BAYERN MUNICH | EINTRACHT FRANKFURT

5 LIVINGSTON FC | CELTIC FC | ST. MIRREN FC | ROSS COUNTY FC

6 DC UNITED | INTER MIAMI CF | CHARLOTTE FC | NEW YORK RED BULLS

TRUE OR FALSE?

1 The English top-flight league schedules all matches on the 25th December for noon.

TRUE ☐ FALSE ☐

2 Petr Čech has the most top-flight clean sheets by a goalie in England.

TRUE ☐ FALSE ☐

3 West Ham's London Stadium was built for the 2012 Olympic Games.

TRUE ☐ FALSE ☐

4 The oldest ever top-flight player in England was Ajay Elder, aged 43.

TRUE ☐ FALSE ☐

5 VAR stands for 'Virtual Assistant Referee' and is used to help referees.

TRUE ☐ FALSE ☐

6 James Milner has played over 600 top-flight league matches in England.

TRUE ☐ FALSE ☐

7 The UEFA Champions League takes place every three seasons.

TRUE ☐ FALSE ☐

8 In the 2021-22 top-flight season, two players hit the post seven times!

TRUE ☐ FALSE ☐

STADIUM DESIGN

CREATE!

Some people prefer traditional football stadiums, while others love huge modern arenas. Use this space to design an awesome stadium for your team!

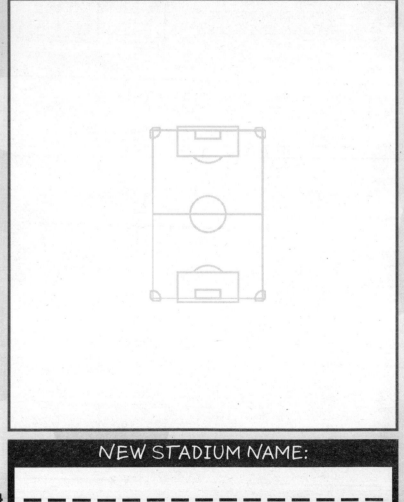

NEW STADIUM NAME:

TACTICAL CODES

DIFFICULTY:

The goalkeeper has had an idea for a counter attack! He's sent a code to his winger and striker. Can you work out what tactical idea they have had?

9   23 9 12 12   8 9 20
9 20   12 15 14 7.   8 5 1 4
9 20   15 22 5 18   20 15
20 8 5   19 20 18 9 11 5 18!

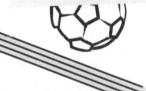

CODE BREAKING RULES

Each number represents where the letter comes in the alphabet. For example, 1 is A, 18 is R and 26 is Z

THE CODED MESSAGE IS:

_ ____ ___ __ __ ____.

____ __ ____ __ __ ____

___ _____!

CARD STATS

DIFFICULTY: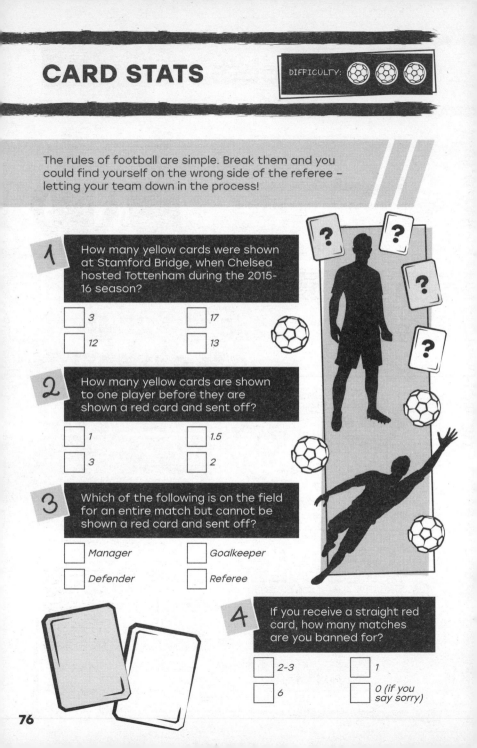

The rules of football are simple. Break them and you could find yourself on the wrong side of the referee – letting your team down in the process!

1 How many yellow cards were shown at Stamford Bridge, when Chelsea hosted Tottenham during the 2015-16 season?

- [ ] 3
- [ ] 12
- [ ] 17
- [ ] 13

2 How many yellow cards are shown to one player before they are shown a red card and sent off?

- [ ] 1
- [ ] 3
- [ ] 1.5
- [ ] 2

3 Which of the following is on the field for an entire match but cannot be shown a red card and sent off?

- [ ] Manager
- [ ] Defender
- [ ] Goalkeeper
- [ ] Referee

4 If you receive a straight red card, how many matches are you banned for?

- [ ] 2-3
- [ ] 6
- [ ] 1
- [ ] 0 (if you say sorry)

5 The most yellow cards received in one English top-flight season was by Leeds in 2021-22. How many did they get?

☐ 101   ☐ 1001   ☐ 199   ☐ 73

6 Liverpool legend Steven Gerrard was once shown a red card after how long?

☐ 1 minutes   ☐ 5 minutes

☐ 9 minutes   ☐ 38 seconds

7 If a player is shown a red card, when does their ban begin?

☐ After 1 week   ☐ Immediately

☐ Next season   ☐ Within 1 month

8 In what year were cards first introduced to the English football leagues?

☐ 2001

☐ 1976

☐ 1995

☐ 1983

9 Who received the fastest English top-flight yellow card, after 15 seconds?

☐ Sadio Mané   ☐ Harry Kane

☐ John Stones   ☐ Declan Rice

10 In the 2021-22 season, which team earned the most red cards (six) in the English top-flight league?

☐ Man City   ☐ West Ham

☐ Everton   ☐ Aston Villa

CARD STATS

Another exciting Match Attax card has been divided into five strips. Your task is to put the card back together. Can you see what order the card needs to go in?

A   B   C   D   E   F

TROPHY CELEBRATION

You've reached the end of the awesome quizzes, puzzles and challenges! As a reward, join the dots below and you'll be awarded an epic trophy to celebrate with!

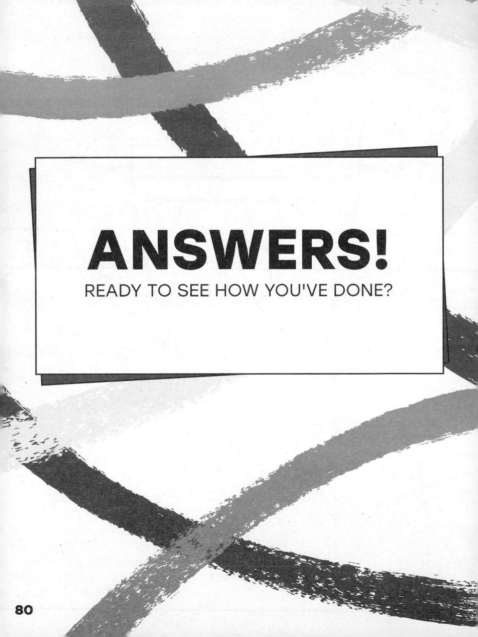

ANSWERS!

READY TO SEE HOW YOU'VE DONE?

PAGE 6-7

1 Cristiano Ronaldo
2 Mohamed Salah
3 Alan Shearer
4 Chloe Kelly
5 7.69

6 5
7 8
8 Manchester City
9 25
10 Marcus Rashford

PAGE 9

EASY

TOUGH

WORLD CLASS

PAGE 10-11

1 False
2 True
3 False
4 False

5 False
6 True
7 True
8 False

START

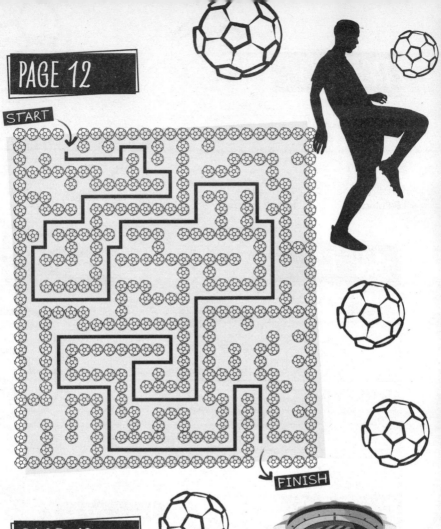

FINISH

PAGE 13

EVERTON FC - THE TOFFEES
LEICESTER CITY - THE FOXES
BRIGHTON & HOVE ALBION - THE SEAGULLS
CRYSTAL PALACE - THE EAGLES
AFC BOURNEMOUTH - THE CHERRIES
WEST HAM UTD - THE HAMMERS
BRENTFORD FC - THE BEES
MANCHESTER UTD - THE RED DEVILS

PAGE 14-15

1 1910
2 Real Madrid
3 Wembley Stadium
4 Borussia Dortmund
5 Fulham
6 Goodison Park
7 Molineux Stadium
8 Paris Saint-Germain
9 Anfield
10 133 metres

PAGE 16

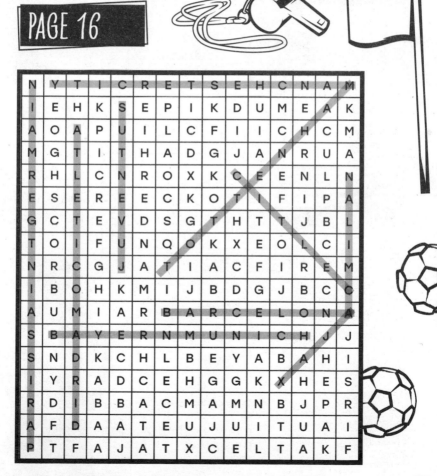

N	Y	T	I	C	R	E	T	S	E	H	C	N	A	M
I	E	H	K	S	E	P	I	K	D	U	M	E	A	K
A	O	A	P	U	I	L	C	F	I	I	C	H	C	M
M	G	T	I	T	H	A	D	G	J	A	N	R	U	A
R	H	L	C	N	R	O	X	K	C	E	E	N	L	N
E	S	E	R	E	E	C	K	O	T	I	F	I	P	A
G	C	T	E	V	D	S	G	T	H	T	T	J	B	L
T	O	I	F	U	N	Q	O	K	X	E	O	L	C	I
N	R	C	G	J	A	T	I	A	C	F	I	R	E	M
I	B	O	H	K	M	I	J	B	D	G	J	B	C	C
A	U	M	I	A	R	B	A	R	C	E	L	O	N	A
S	B	A	Y	E	R	N	M	U	N	I	C	H	J	J
S	N	D	K	C	H	L	B	E	Y	A	B	A	H	I
I	Y	R	A	D	C	E	H	G	G	K	X	H	E	S
R	D	I	B	B	A	C	M	A	M	N	B	J	P	R
A	F	D	A	A	T	E	U	J	U	I	T	U	A	I
P	T	F	A	J	A	T	X	C	E	L	T	A	K	F

GK Ederson   **CM** Foden   **RF** Kane
RB Walker   **CM** Mount   **CF** Haaland
CB van Dijk   **RW** Bellingham   **LF** Mbappé
LB Alaba   **LW** Raphinha

Across/Down crossword:

- 5 VAR
- 6 PUNCH
- 7 ASSISTANT
- 8 SOCCER
- 1 PRESS
- 2 SUBSTITUTE
- 3 TACTICS
- 4 RED

1 Thiago Silva   **6** Tyrick Mitchell
2 France   **7** 0
3 Wigan Athletic   **8** Trent Alexander-Arnold
4 Gary Neville   **9** Barcelona
5 2018   **10** 2

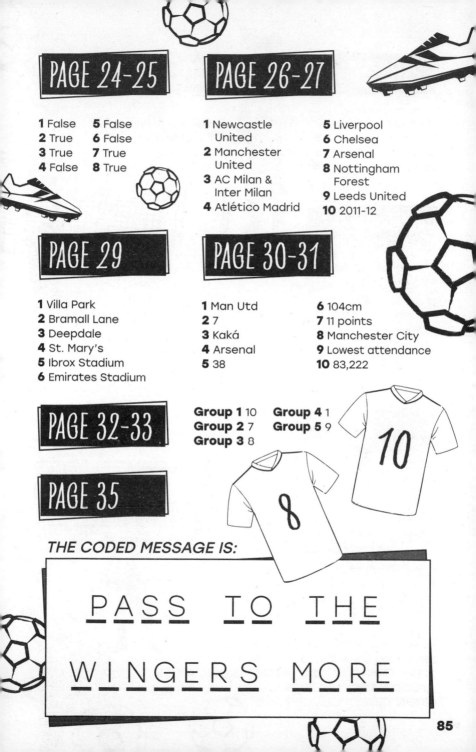

PAGE 24-25

1 False	**5** False
2 True	**6** False
3 True	**7** True
4 False	**8** True

PAGE 26-27

1 Newcastle United	**5** Liverpool
2 Manchester United	**6** Chelsea
3 AC Milan & Inter Milan	**7** Arsenal
4 Atlético Madrid	**8** Nottingham Forest
	9 Leeds United
	10 2011-12

PAGE 29

1 Villa Park
2 Bramall Lane
3 Deepdale
4 St. Mary's
5 Ibrox Stadium
6 Emirates Stadium

PAGE 30-31

1 Man Utd	**6** 104cm
2 7	**7** 11 points
3 Kaká	**8** Manchester City
4 Arsenal	**9** Lowest attendance
5 38	**10** 83,222

PAGE 32-33

Group 1 10	**Group 4** 1
Group 2 7	**Group 5** 9
Group 3 8	

PAGE 35

THE CODED MESSAGE IS:

PASS TO THE WINGERS MORE

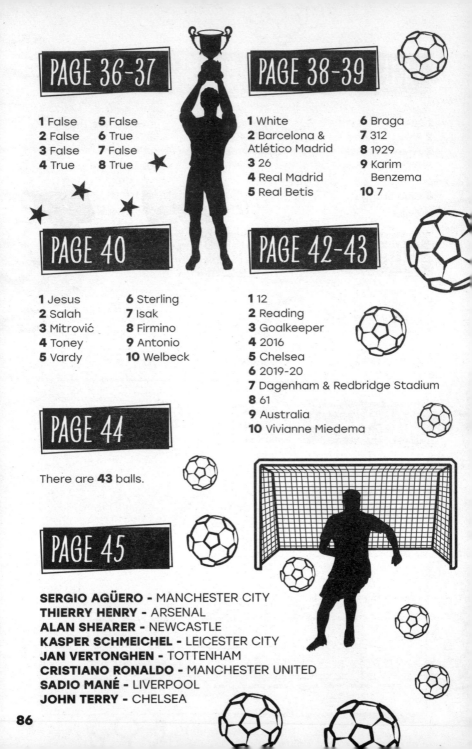

PAGE 36-37

1 False   **5** False
2 False   **6** True
3 False   **7** False
4 True   **8** True

PAGE 38-39

1 White   **6** Braga
2 Barcelona &   **7** 312
Atlético Madrid   **8** 1929
3 26   **9** Karim
4 Real Madrid   Benzema
5 Real Betis   **10** 7

PAGE 40

1 Jesus   **6** Sterling
2 Salah   **7** Isak
3 Mitrović   **8** Firmino
4 Toney   **9** Antonio
5 Vardy   **10** Welbeck

PAGE 42-43

1 12
2 Reading
3 Goalkeeper
4 2016
5 Chelsea
6 2019-20
7 Dagenham & Redbridge Stadium
8 61
9 Australia
10 Vivianne Miedema

PAGE 44

There are **43** balls.

PAGE 45

SERGIO AGÜERO - MANCHESTER CITY
THIERRY HENRY - ARSENAL
ALAN SHEARER - NEWCASTLE
KASPER SCHMEICHEL - LEICESTER CITY
JAN VERTONGHEN - TOTTENHAM
CRISTIANO RONALDO - MANCHESTER UNITED
SADIO MANÉ - LIVERPOOL
JOHN TERRY - CHELSEA

PAGE 46-47

1 28
2 34
3 Troyes
4 He has played for and managed PSG
5 Club Brugge

6 120
7 Sergio Agüero
8 4
9 Marseille
10 2017

PAGE 49

B   C   A   E   F   D

MASON MOUNT CHELSEA

MID

POWER PLAY
85

8.0M

DEFENCE
57

ATTACK
83

100 CLUB

PAGE 50-51

1 10
2 Bayern Munich
3 312
4 17

5 1963
6 Borussia Dortmund
7 Winter break
8 Bruno Fernandes

9 2009
10 Graham Potter

PAGE 52

START

NO GOAL

NO GOAL

NO GOAL

NO GOAL

NO GOAL

NO GOAL

NO GOAL

NO GOAL

GOAL!

P	G	P	C	R	M	Z	Q	N	K
D	L	E	U	K	I	X	J	I	M
G	U	H	N	T	N	E	R	A	I
R	F	S	Z	G	E	B	W	U	M
E	X	Q	K	W	Y	L	V	N	E
B	R	O	N	Z	E	R	L	T	A
R	R	M	P	P	O	P	B	A	D
E	E	D	C	M	B	I	N	R	S
G	C	M	I	E	D	E	M	A	Y
E	R	E	N	A	R	D	Q	Z	J
H	W	H	A	U	A	T	R	A	M

1 False   **5** True
2 True   **6** False
3 False   **7** False
4 False   **8** True

Player 1
Chloe Kelly
Player 2
Kevin De Bruyne
Player 3
Pierre-Emerick
Aubameyang
Player 4
Lionel Messi

1 105
2 11
3 Arsenal
4 Benfica
5 91,648
6 Erling Haaland
7 Porto
8 Liverpool
9 It was played in August
10 September

PAGE 60

Crossword answers:

Across:
6 HENDERSON
7 JORGINHO
8 GREALISH

Down:
1 HØJBJERG
2 FERNANDES
3 PEDRI
4 KIMMICH
5 SILVA

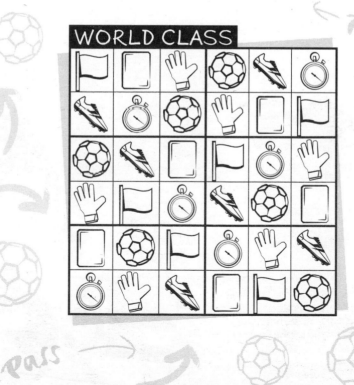

PAGE 64-65

1 Martin Odegaard

2 Skipper

3 Vice captain

4 Croatia

5 Defender

6 Fernandinho

7 Tottenham Hotspur

8 Hugo Lloris

9 Flip a coin

10 2007

ERIC DIER

His team is **England** (not Scotland).

ÉDOUARD MENDY

His team is **Chelsea** (not Arsenal).

BRUNO GUIMARÃES

His team is **Newcastle** (not Aston Villa).

DECLAN RICE

His top-flight league debut was **2017** (not 2020).

CHRISTIAN ERIKSEN

He was born in **1992** (not 2002).

JAMES WARD-PROWSE

His position is **midfielder** (not defender).

1 Community Shield
2 Ribbons
3 Captain
4 Quarter finals
5 Germany
6 A treble
7 1871
8 2018-19
9 Silverware
10 A medal

PAGE 71

1 Real Madrid
2 Manchester City
3 Paris Saint-Germain
4 Bayern Munich
5 Celtic FC
6 DC United

PAGE 72-73

1 False
2 True
3 True
4 False
5 False
6 True
7 False (takes place every season)
8 True (Raphinha and Mbeumo)

PAGE 75

THE CODED MESSAGE IS:

I WILL HIT IT LONG.

HEAD IT OVER TO

THE STRIKER!

E   D   F   B   A   C

MATCH ATTAX — TRADING CARD GAME

Topps

FOR

POWER PLAY
91

9.5M

VINI JR. REAL MADRID

DEFENCE
35

ATTACK
90

100 CLUB